MW01594759

A SPIRIT DAUGHTER WORKBOOK

written by
Jill Wintersteen

FOR THE CAPRICORN SEASON

+

THE SOLAR ECLIPSE
Wednesday, December 25th
9:13PM PST

Thursday, December 26th
2:13AM UTC

This Workbook is designed to be used throughout the Season of Capricorn and during her Solar Eclipse. Use pages 2-15 + 30-34 from December 21st until January 19th to help you align with the Seasonal Sun Energy of Capricorn. Use pages 16-29 during the days around the Capricorn Solar Eclipse, December 25th, to harness her power to create a new reality.

CAPRICORN

Each zodiac season is an evolution of the one before it. As we follow along with the stars and the Sun, we gain an opportunity to transform and refine our energy each Season. Where Sagittarius broadened our views and perspectives, Capricorn re-centers our focus to what is truly worth our attention. This is the Season to create clear intentions around who you are and what you want to do with your time. Capricorn's energy brings us sheer determination and teaches us that we are capable of accomplishing any goal and living any dream. Nothing is too challenging or too ambitious in the Season of the sea-goat. Capricorn reminds us that no matter what life brings us, we have the fortitude to meet it and can rise to any level demanded of us. In many ways, this is the Season to feel our inherent power and learn to believe in ourselves and our visions.

Made of Earth and ruled by the planet of responsibility, Saturn, Capricorn brings a certain gravitas to the zodiac. There is a seriousness to this Season as we realize another year is upon us and with it, vast potential but limited time. This Season is a time to contemplate what is worth our focus, our determination, and our precious resources. What warrants your full attention, and furthermore, what captures it amidst the constant distractions this world offers? We live amongst unlimited possibilities. We can be anyone, pursue any dream, and live any life we desire. Amid all the possible experiences you could live, which one speaks to your inner truths? Which one aligns with who you are at your core and is the most authentic manifestation of your soul?

More than any other sign, Capricorn reminds us that we have a responsibility in this lifetime. A responsibility to understand who we are, including what we value, what we stand for, and what we believe is fair to ourselves and others. The energy of Capricorn aligns us with our integrity and helps us define it. It brings us back to the center of our being and helps us strengthen the foundation we build everything else upon. Over this Season ask yourself what truths create the basis of your being? What do you honor in yourself, and how can you continue to hold your integrity in every situation? Part of this Season is merging your inner world and your outer one. Do you share the most valued pieces of yourself with the world? Or do you hide them behind a mask put on for the approval of others?

Once we understand who we are and gain the courage to show up as that person in every area of our life, we find our passion and our passion can then become our life's work. Capricorn teaches us that when we align our work with who we are at our core, magic occurs. Our path unfolds in front of us, and all the support we need appears at the right moment. We attract situations, people and opportunities that help us in doing the job only we can do. We are filled with purpose, and that purpose becomes pure joy.

Finding our life's work takes time, though. It takes hours spent in quiet contemplation with our soul, a commitment to pursue our dreams, and balance with the rest of our life to prevent depletion. Capricorn Season begins each year on the Winter Solstice, for those of us in the Northern Hemisphere. Winter naturally pulls our energy inward and encourages us to sit with ourselves. The long nights and cold mornings set the perfect stage for introspection. Over this Season, dedicate yourself to practices that help you understand yourself and hear your inner wisdom. Create routines for yourself, which both nourish you and focus your energy. Each day, decide where you want to dedicate your energy. Be honest with yourself about how much you have to give to projects, people, and yourself. Then align with Capricorn to discern how to spend your energetic currency. Decide how to spend your time and allow what you love doing to shine on the many paths you could take. Continually ask yourself what is worth your energy, and by the end of Capricorn Season, you'll have a clear answer and an illuminated path.

MOONSCOPES

Moonscopes are based on your Moon Sign. They provide guidance and insight about how your personal Moon, otherwise known as your emotions, will be affected by the Seasonal energy of Capricorn. These energies will amplify on her New Moon.

Aries Moon: You love excitement and change. You need to feel life living through you to be content. Allow the Season of Capricorn to inspire you to direct some of your fire and motivation towards one intention. Challenge yourself to commit to a practice that helps you stay grounded and rooted in yourself. Feel the freshness of this Season and harness it to create a new reality from dedication and focused work. On the New Moon, ask yourself: "How can I ignite my passions this year and create a plan to follow through on what I start?"

Taurus Moon: You thrive with routines and schedules, as they comfort your heart. You also need to feel secure in every aspect of your life, including your work life. Feel into the stability of Capricorn Season. Create new practices that bring you home to yourself every day. As you connect more deeply with your center, challenge yourself to take some risks, knowing that you can always rely on yourself. On the New Moon, ask yourself: "How can I experience new adventures this year, while still feeling safe and at ease?"

Gemini Moon: You love the social aspect of life, and this time of year brings plenty of opportunities for you to exchange energy with others. Be aware of burning out, though, as you need just as much rest as activity. Ground yourself through practices that focus your curious mind and center your energy. In this clear space, create new ways to communicate your thoughts and vibrations. Carry these creations into the New Year and use them to nourish your roots when life begins to feel scattered. On the New Moon, ask yourself: "How can I express myself in new ways, while staying centered in my core?"

Cancer Moon: This time of year can often feel unsettling to you, as you like to spend time with yourself and feel most secure at home. Spend time with people who understand your need to explore every nuance life offers and support you in taking care of yourself. As we shift into the later part of Capricorn Season, feel the stability of new routines helping to nourish your heart and create space for you to feel even more deeply. On the New Moon, ask yourself: "How can I create practices which take care of my soul, but also allow me to be supported by others?"

Leo Moon: You love to find new ways to share your unique talents with others. Allow Capricorn Season to inspire you to create new ways of showing up in the world that speak directly from your heart. Experiment with expressing yourself, and your talents, in new forms. You are often loyal to everyone around you, be loyal to yourself this Season, and dedicate yourself to practices that bring out your natural creativity. On the New Moon, ask yourself," "How can I express my authentic truth in new ways which allow me to lead myself and others?"

Virgo Moon: You love to be of service to others, and often make it part of your life's work. You also love organization and schedules, which allow you to make the most of your time and energy. Feel Capricorn Season inspiring you to discern what projects, people, and activities are worth your precious time. Create practices that help you grow, feel your progress, and align with your soul. As you reaffirm your center, feel how you can share it with the world through your work. On the New Moon, ask yourself: "What practices will nourish me so I can nourish others?"

*You can look up your Moon Sign at astro-charts.com

MOONSCOPES

Libra Moon: You love to feel at peace with yourself and your environment. This time of year can throw your natural equilibrium off balance and scatter your energy. Align with Capricorn Season to recenter yourself through daily practices like meditation or creating art. You have a natural tendency towards creating beauty everywhere around you, nurture this part throughout Capricorn Season. Find new ways to show your creations to the world, incorporating them with your life's work. On the New Moon, ask yourself: "How can I teach my heart serenity while finding my place in the world?"

Scorpio Moon: You love to plunge deeply into your psyche and understand yourself on every level. You never shy away from any feeling but tend to keep them close to your heart. Feel into the structure and containers Capricorn Season brings to your emotions. Create routines and practices which help you focus on unraveling your energy and give you space to bring it back together. As you work with your energy, feel how your very process can feed into your life's work and how you show up for others. On the New Moon, ask yourself: "How can I create space for myself to feel and use those feelings to fuel my work?"

Sagittarius Moon: You crave adventure and freedom. You thrive in novel experiences where you need faith and trust to navigate your way through. Capricorn Season may feel a little dull to your senses but can provide some necessary grounding for your energy. Feel into the structure this Season offers to create a stable foundation for you to leap from in the New Year. Create practices that allow you to feel free but also recenter your energy. On the New Moon, ask yourself: "How can I remain expansive while focusing my energy on my intentions?"

Capricorn Moon: You are at home this Season and New Moon. You thrive with routine and organization in your life. You also need quiet time alone to contemplate the depths of your soul. You are the definition of "still waters run deep," and this is your Season to feel your stable center. Create time for yourself and dedicate yourself to disciples which help you feel your home frequency. Align with your authentic truths and values, then align them with your life's work. On the New Moon, ask yourself: "What practices heighten your intuition and give you space to follow it?"

Aquarius Moon: You crave independence and individual self-expression. You can be quite eccentric and need different methods to explore your unique perspectives. Throughout Capricorn Season, create practices that encourage expanding your already expansive perspectives. Experiment with new ways of thinking and being as we start the New Year. Recognize your talent to see what others do not have the capacity for at this time and bring your progressive ideas into your work. On the New Moon, ask yourself: "How can I understand my unique talents to a greater degree, and share them with the collective?"

Pisces Moon: You crave to understand your own soul, and consciousness, on a deeper level. Often this exploration comes through time spent in meditation, breathwork exercises, or other means, which bring you in direct contact with your energy. Align with the structure of Capricorn Season to create a routine around the practices which support the exploration of your soul. Realize that this is serious work you are doing, not just a hobby or a way to pass the time. You can understand energy dynamics in a profound way, unavailable to others. Once you have unraveled some of the mysteries of being human, find ways to share them with the world through creative expressions of your consciousness.

*You can look up your Moon Sign at astro-charts.com

CRYSTALS FOR CAPRICORN

Fluorite is a wonderful stone to help you focus. It increases your ability to concentrate on a task and assists in new learning. It will help you look at any situation with a discerning and objective eye. Use it when you are taking on something new or when you need to review information without preconceived bias. Fluorite is also a powerful stone for clearing negativity both energetically and physically. Use it when you feel others have influenced your emotions or when you feel a cold coming on. It will clear out energies that do not belong to you. Fluorite is either green, purple, or clear and often comes in a cubed formation.

Fluorite vibrates to the Mantra: "I am focused."

Garnet is a powerful stone used for many things, including grounding your energy. Wear some around your ankle on days when you have lots to do and think about, as it will control your racing mind. You can also wear it on your right hand, as it will stimulate the masculine side of your body, helping you tap into your logical intuition. Garnet is also known as a stone for commitment, helping you fully devote yourself to a project, person, or even yourself. When deciding where you should plant your flag, have some near you, or hold some in your hand. Garnet is dark red.

Garnet vibrates to the Mantra, "I am grounded."

Bloodstone is an excellent stone for deep contemplation. It facilitates concentration and can boost mental activity so decisions come with more ease. Have it near you during meditation when you a have a choice to make, then watch the answers magically appear. It's also a great stone to boost your immune system, as it improves physical strength and endurance. If you feel a cold or the flu coming on, lay some on your chest as you rest. Bloodstone is dark green with a speck of red.

Bloodstone vibrates to the Mantra: "I am strong."

Hematite is known as the stone for the mind. It helps increase mental activity as well as discernment. It will help you sort things out in your life and make changes where they are necessary. It is also a very grounding stone, helping to clear your mind. Its natural magnetic pull aligns the body, mind, and spirit, bringing you balance. Hematite is silver.

Hematite vibrates to the Mantra: "I am discerning."

Malachite is a stone of transformation. It helps to create an energetic barrier around the wearer during times of dynamic shifting. Through this boundary, Malachite facilitates creativity and deep intuition that comes from a place within, uninfluenced by the opinions of others. Have some on you, or near, when you need to access answers from your inner depths. Through tuning into the power of your higher guidance, you will stay grounded as vibrations shift around you. Malachite is green with beautiful swirls of darker green.

Malachite vibrates to the Mantra: "I am transforming."

CAPRICORN LUNAR FLOW

Capricorn provides us with very grounded energy, creating stillness and focus. During her season, harness this energy within by practicing yoga postures that connect you to this Earth energy. Capricorn also rules the knees, joints, teeth, and skeletal system. Take care of these body parts during her season, especially the knees. This following sequence is designed to help you feel grounded and throughout your body and mind.

Joint Series

Be free with your body in these series. Practice each part for however long feels comfortable to you. Begin in a comfortable seated position. Have your spine straight and support your hips, or knees if needed. Begin by slowing rolling your neck in one direction, making large circles. After a few breaths, switch directions. Bring your head back to center, then shrug your shoulders up and back for a few breaths before switching direction, rolling them forward. Roll them back one more time, then come to stillness. Next, begin to stretch your jaw. Open it wide, then close a couple of times to release tension often held here. After your jaw is relaxed, extend your arms out to either side. Make a circle with your wrist about 3-5 times in one direction, then switch your rotation. You can even roll your finger around will you rotate the wrists. Lower your arms, then begin to rotate your torso in one direction feeling your spine begin to loosen. After about 3-5 spins, switch directions. Come to stillness, then begin to arch and flex your spine as you would in Cat/Cow. Keep your abdominal slightly drawn in to protect your low back. Keep this up for about 5 rounds, or however much you need.

Come to hands and knees, making sure your knees are properly padded. Step your right foot forward for a low lunge. Keep your hands on the ground. Flex into the right knee, moving your hips forward, then straighten the front leg out, pushing your hips back. Move with the breath here, exhaling to bend, inhaling to straighten. Continue this 5 times, then switch sides.

Come back to a seated position with your legs extended straight. Sit on a pillow or bolster to straighten your spine. Begin to make circles with your feet, rotating your ankles in one direction. After a few rounds, switch sides. Finally, point and flex your feet a few times, stretching the top of the ankles. After you've finished, take a mini savasana to allow your body to fully integrate the movements. You can practice this sequence alone, or with the rest of the poses.

CAPRICORN LUNAR FLOW

Mountain Pose

Stand at the top of the mat, feet together, with eyes closed. Root your feet into the ground as you breathe deeply, rising tall through the crown of your head. Inhale for a count of 4, exhale for a count of 4. Repeat this breath for about a minute as you feel into your body and the present moment.

Half Moon Standing Variation

Open your eyes, and on your inhale, reach your arms overhead. Clasp the left wrist with the right hand. On exhale side bend to the right, keeping a firm footing on the ground. Breathe with the same 4 count breath here for 5 breaths, lengthening through the left side. On inhale, lift the torso and slowly switch sides.

Forward Bend

Inhale, reach the arms overhead; on exhale slowly fold forward hinging at the hips. Press your feet into the ground and firm up your legs as you let the torso and neck relax. Feel the strength of your lower body as you release your upper body for 5 breaths.

Warrior 1 > Warrior 2 > Wide Angle Forward Bend > Warrior 2 > Warrior 1

From the top of your mat, step your right foot back into Warrior 1. Have the back foot angled at a 45-degree angle as you bend into the front knee. Reach your arms up overhead as you breathe for 4 counts on inhale and exhale. Hold for 5 breaths then, on Exhale, open up the hips to the right for Warrior 2. Reach your arms out to either side and adjust your back foot out a bit. Bend into the front knee, breathing deeply as you focus your attention on your front hand. Take 5 breaths here, stretching the hips. On inhale, straighten the front leg and parallel the feet for a wide-angled forward bend. With your hands on your hips, inhale and reach the spine upward, then exhale and fold over your legs. Release your hands to the ground and breathe for 5 longs breaths, firming up through the legs. On inhale, place your hands on the hips and come back up to standing. Turn the right foot forward and repeat Warrior 1 and 2 on this side.

Tree Pose

Float your eyes open and press down into your left foot. Slowly bring the right foot up for tree pose, placing it on the inside of the left leg. Press firmly down through your standing leg, imagining roots going down into the Earth, providing you with balance. Reach and lengthen your spine upward, growing taller through your torso as you lift your arms to the sky. Take 5 deep breaths here before switching sides.

Forward Bend

After tree pose, slowly come down to seated. Place a blanket or pillow under your hips and extend your legs out in front of you. Flex through the feet and straighten out through your legs. Inhale and reach your arms up to the sky. As you exhale, fold over your legs as you lengthen through your back. With every inhale, reach through your spine, and with every exhale, fold a bit deeper. Stay here for 5-7 breaths, feeling the ground beneath you and allowing your mind to settle.

Twist

Come up slowly from the forward bend and lay down on your back. Gently hug both knees into the chest. Twist them over the right as you extend out through the arms. Expand your ribs on each inhale and on exhale twist deeper. Spend 5 breaths here, and then lift them back up and over the other side.

Savasana- 5 mins.

*Bonus for the Eclipse. Place a few drops of Rose Oil on your forehead during Savasana, to help calm and ground your energy. Extend both legs out on the ground. Feel your body completely supported and allow this support to relax your body and mind. Return to a natural breath and simply observe the flow of inhale and exhale as you rest.

CAPRICORN MEDITATION

Capricorn reminds us that we are always connected to the Earth. At any moment, we can align our vibrations with the support and structure of Mother Gaia. The following meditation is designed to help you plug back into the Earth to feel supported, nourished, and energetically integrated. The Earth also provides a space or us to shed unwanted energies. Try to practice this meditation for the entire Capricorn season, and especially on the Solar Eclipse. Align with the energy of Capricorn when you feel spaced out, restless, or unable to concentrate. Nourish your connection with the Earth and nourish the connection with yourself.

Grounding Cord Meditation - 10 mins

Begin in a seated posture, switching your leg position if needed. Close your eyes and imagine a white cord extending from the base of your tailbone into the Earth far below you. Even if you are on the second or third floor, see the cord plugging deep into the Earth. As you inhale, feel energy running up the cord through your spine to the crown of your head. On exhale, send energy back into the Earth through the cord, connecting your field with that of the Earth. Inhale as nourishing Earth energy moves up through the cord, exhale, reconnect your frequency to the Earth. You may breathe as fast or slow as you like. Feel your body relax, including your shoulders and neck, as you allow the Earth to support you through this cord. Know this connection is available to you at any time; it is just a matter of placing your attention on the ground, which is always present. After you finish, slowly open your eyes and allow the light to reenter. Feel yourself centered in your body and energy. As you move through the rest of the day, remember that you are one with Earth, her stability is also yours.

Vajrasattva Mantra

The Vajrasttva Mantra is a Tibetan Buddhist practice done to help purify the energetic field. Try practicing this Mantra on the day of the New Moon/Solar Eclipse as a way to clear yourself of energetic ties and make space for new vibrations to enter your field. This Mantra holds the power to open up the gateway between the heart and mind, helping to keep intentions clear and focused. It is always best to chant mantras 108 times. You may use a mala bead necklace to help you keep count, saying one chant per bead. You may also chant this Mantra 54 or 27 times. It is encouraged that you use a recording to learn the Mantra before chanting it. You can find plenty of examples of this Mantra on YouTube or through Deva Premal.

Before you begin, find a comfortable seated position. If possible, practice this Mantra during the actual times of the Eclipse from 7:34PMm PST - 11:00 PM PST. Close your eyes and clear your mind. You can repeat the Mantra out loud or to yourself. Repeat the phrase "Om Benza Satto Hung" 108 times. Once you have finished sit for five minutes in silence and feel the vibration of the Mantra integrating into your energy field. Feel it detaching you from old karma and making space for new intentions and patterns to enter.

ALIGNING the SPIRIT

Tips for Focusing Your Energy

"Start each day visualizing what you want.
Then say no to anything that isn't it."

- spirit daughter

Knowing where to place our energy is not always easy. There are endless possibilities available to each of us, and we really do have the ability to manifest anything we want. With all of the potential lives we could live, the challenge becomes choosing the one we truly want. It is hard to attract the energy we need to manifest our dreams if we are not clear in our intentions. The universe can't give us something that we don't even know we want. Below are some tips to help you focus your energy first, then hone in on what exactly you want to call into your world. Practice these before writing your intentions, as they will help you become even more detailed in your dreams. Energy loves details; the more specific you are with your intentions, the likelihood of manifesting them quickly increases.

Visualize Your Day

The power of intention is not just for the New Moon. You can bring it into your life daily through morning visualization of how you want your day to unfold. Each morning take a moment to close your eyes and see your day as if you are watching a movie. See yourself accomplishing everything you desire. Allow yourself to feel like the day has already happened and be grateful for the energetic support helping you to manifest it. Continue your visualizations by writing down three things that would raise your vibration throughout the day. This could be a walk, or talking to a friend, or accomplishing a goal, or merely resting. Hold your visions throughout the day and challenge yourself not to do anything which doesn't align with them.

Learn to Say No

At any given point, we have countless energies fighting for our attention. This can be your partner, your job, your parents, or even the energy of a new project. To truly focus your energy, you must learn to say no- without guilt. Many of us struggle with the simple word "no" even with ourselves. We negotiate, we vacillate between decisions, and we waste time. If it's not a resounding yes, it's a no. This is where your intuition can help. Most of us have had an idea presented to us at some point and heard the little voice inside screaming no, only to say maybe or worse, yes. When we say yes when we mean no, we feel drained energetically because we did not listen to ourselves. We did not honor ourselves, which is far worse than letting someone else down. If that little voice within says no, say it on the outside. Then congratulate yourself for respecting the sacred contact with your spirit.

ALIGNING the SPIRIT

Know Your Distractions

Distractions- we all have them. They come in many forms; social media, shopping, eating, even certain relationships can be distractions in the moment. It's ok to have distractions; our brain actually needs them to provide a break from the task at hand. Used wisely, distractions can improve our focus because they provide a moment of recharge. First, though, we must be aware of our "go-to" diversion tactics. Make a list of your common distractions and notice when you rely on them the most. Start by limiting the time you spend with them by creating boundaries for yourself, especially when you know you like the distraction.

Write the 5/5 Daily

This daily exercise is recommended for the week leading up to the New Moon, as it will help you craft your intentions. You can also continue this practice daily throughout the year as a way to check in with yourself and the dreams you are pursuing. Create two lists. On the first list, write five things you need to do today. This can be anything from "pick up dry cleaning" to "write a blog post." As you write these tasks, notice how you feel about them, i.e., are you happy with your current daily life. A great life is found in the details. We may not like everything we do every day, but the goal is to love most of what you do day today. For the second list, write five things you want to do in your life. These can be anything, and you don't need to worry about how you will get there. They can be anything from "be on Oprah" to "sail around the world." They may also be something like "feel content with my life." or "be appreciated." As you continue to write these lists, notice the things which remain consistent in the second list. If "sail the world" shows up on your list for a week, or even a year, then perhaps focus your energy on learning how to sail or at least on saving the money to buy a dependable boat. Have fun with the second list. Let your mind wander to things you may have never considered. Then be open to these new dreams sticking around. When they do, adjust your course to include them and recognize you just learned where to focus your energy.

Feel Your Dreams

You may find your list of desires changes every day, and you don't know which dream you want. This uncertainty is natural. It's also natural to want something one day, then get it, only to find out you want something different. Often we need to "try on" different dreams before we can know which one is best. We can do this by actually trying them out, or we can get a taste of how our body and energy reacts to the vision through daydreaming. Even when our mind can't decide, our bodies never lie.

Say you want a new job, but you're unsure of where you want to work. You have two companies in mind, maybe more. Sit back and allow your body to relax. Before you start the practice, do a quick body scan by mentally going through your body from head to toes. Notice any existing tension. Don't try to change anything; just notice what is already present in your energy. Now begin to imagine, in detail, a day of work at the first company. After you've gone through your imaginary day, go back to the body scan and notice if anything has changed. Observe any new tension or the release of previous tension. Feel how your body reacted to the dream, were there any blocks or openings? Take a few breaths to reset, then start the process for the second dream. Afterward, compare how you felt in the two different scenarios. Your body can tell you a lot of things, like when something doesn't fully resonate with you or where fear is hiding. Spend time exploring and use this information from your energetic field to form your intentions.

PERSONAL SIGNS

People with their Sun in Capricorn are resourceful, reliable, and independent. They are excellent workers and commit with ease to any project they feel is worth their valuable attention. They have a laser-sharp focus and often can cut through the fluff of life straight to the heart of the matter. They have little tolerance for drama and have no problem walking away from situations or people who create disturbances in their world.

Capricorn Suns need time alone, often in nature. They need to continually recenter themselves and remind themselves of their authentic truths. They can be perceived as aloof by those around them, but they need time to connect with themselves without the distraction of others. Capricorn Suns are happiest when they have something to focus on, especially in the form of work. They may spend years trying to find a career that fulfills them and captures their active mind, but once they do find their path, they commit for life.

They do, however, need to be aware of burn out and exhaustion. Capricorn Suns tend to work late into the night, often forgetting to nourish themselves as they get lost in their tasks. They must continually balance their desire to work with the rest of their life. Capricorn Suns need joy and play just as much as everyone else. They need to make space for these things in their life even if it means they don't achieve everything on their to-do list.

Capricorn Moon Sign

People with their Moon in Capricorn have steady emotions. They often become the rock in most relationships, finding their friends and loved ones relying on them for stability. They are rational in their feelings and don't often get swept away by emotions. They also don't allow their feelings to influence major life decisions. They move from a place of logic and reason, even though their intuition is powerful. They can have a hard time, though, trusting their inner knowledge and can benefit from following it from time to time to experience its accuracy.

Capricorn Moons also need time alone to restore and nourish themselves. They need proper boundaries with all of those around them. They do well in relationships, often committing for life, once their partners understand and do not take offense to their need for alone time. Capricorn Moons need for space does not reflect their feelings for others. It is merely a necessity for their emotional survival.

WINTER SOLSTICE

DEC 21ST

The winter solstice ushers in a period of introspection and focus. It's a time when nature surrenders to stillness as roots are nourished in preparation for Spring. Align with the energy of this day and the start of Capricorn Season by releasing what distracts you from your core and blocks you from focusing on what's most important to your growth. As you become more aware of what absorbs your energy, it becomes easier to decide what's worth your time and energy. Clear space today to gain clarity for the upcoming season and year.

I AM RELEASING
THIS DISTRACTION   TO FOCUS ON

_____ ⟶ _____

_____ ⟶ _____

_____ ⟶ _____

_____ ⟶ _____

_____ ⟶ _____

_____ ⟶ _____

_____ ⟶ _____

SOLAR ECLIPSE

DECEMBER 25TH/DECEMBER 26TH

NORTH NODE IN..	FOCUS ON...
ARIES	Finding courage to pursue your personal journey by releasing the need for status in a career.
TAURUS	Embracing your natural abilities to create and share your work by releasing the need for validation from others.
GEMINI	Developing your communication and dialogue with others by releasing judgment which blocks you from truly hearing another.
CANCER	Learning to trust the power of your intuition by releasing the need for logic and proof.
LEO	Finding new forms of self-expression which feel good to your soul by releasing self- judgment.
VIRGO	Aligning with your life's work through serving others and by releasing any need for recognition.
LIBRA	Creating lasting mutual partnerships which benefit each person's life purpose by releasing the need to "do it all" yourself.
SCORPIO	Embracing personal growth and transformation by releasing the need for financial success. Open yourself to receiving support instead.
SAGITTARIUS	Creating a life which includes travel, expansion and new perspectives by releasing the need for stability and routines.
CAPRICORN	Aligning with what brings you joy by releasing perspectives which focus on struggle and hardship.
AQUARIUS	Expressing yourself to the collective and collaborating with others by releasing the need to hide your feelings.
PISCES	Healing old wounds and receiving the gifts of your intuition by releasing the need for perfection.

SOLAR ECLIPSE

DECEMBER 25TH/DECEMBER 26TH

A powerful Annual Solar Eclipse accompanies the Capricorn New Moon. This type of Eclipse occurs when the Moon moves in front of the Sun, but does not entirely cover it, leaving a ring of fire in the sky. The Maximum Eclipse occurs at 9:17 pm Pacific Time, December 25th. Meaning, for much of the world, it will happen on December 26th. If you live on the East Coast, the Eclipse occurs at 12:17 am December 26th. Although the beauty of this Eclipse will only be seen from Saudi Arabia, Southern India, Parts of Indonesia, Eastern Europe, Western Asia, and northwest Australia, its effects will be felt throughout the world. We can all tap into the energy and vibrations available on a Solar Eclipse.

Solar Eclipses occur on New Moons, supercharging our intentions. Lunar Eclipses occur on Full Moons, amplifying our ability to release. Eclipses become possible when the Moon and the Sun are near the Lunar Nodes. The North and South Lunar Node exist where the Sun's path and the Moon's orbit intersect. They are energetic vortices full of magic and potential. Currently, the North Node is located in the Sign of Cancer, while the South Node sits in opposition in Capricorn.

The North Node pulls the energy of society towards that direction. The North Node holds the lessons humanity is learning and integrating during a certain period of time. The North Node's position in Cancer is pulling the frequency of the planet into understanding the power of femininity and nurturance. It is helping us integrate the foundations of self-care into our daily life while inspiring us to embrace our intuition over our logical mind. The South Node represents what the collective is evolving away from and often illuminates vibrations we have already mastered as a society. The South Node's position in Capricorn inspires us to embrace a softer approach with ourselves and with others. Instead of forcing our way through with logic, the Universe is asking us to feel our way through life with intuition and inner knowledge. The current position of the Lunar Nodes is ushering in a period of self-nourishment, where we can leave behind our workaholic ways for a new paradigm of restoration. It is asking us to be more gentle, more kind, and more willing to feel good instead of busy.

When the Moon and Sun are positioned within 17 degrees of either Node, an Eclipse becomes possible. On our current New Moon, both the Sun and Moon fall close to the South Node in Capricorn, helping us to work with the energy of both Lunar Nodes and set intentions around embracing their higher vibrations. This Eclipse invites us to heal places within our soul which search for hardship. It asks us to redefine what success means and acknowledge that we don't have to work so hard for life to be wonderful. Instead, as we align with the North Node in Cancer, we can redefine how we receive gifts and energy. The current position of the Lunar Nodes is encouraging us to open ourselves to energies always available to us. There s no need to earn them or stress ourselves out to obtain them. We simply need to take care of ourselves and be open to attracting what is already ours.

Along with the collective Nodal positions, we each have a personal North and South Node. You can look yours up at astro-charts.com. The location of your North Node highlights the lessons you are here to learn in this lifetime. The position of your South Node shows the energies you've come into this world already knowing. It is your place of comfort, but also the place which can block your evolution if you become attached to its familiarity.

On this Solar Eclipse, there is an opportunity to integrate the higher vibrations of your personal North Node through reframing the way you experience the energies of the current South Node in Capricorn. To the left is a simple guide on what to work on this Solar Eclipse based on where your North Node is located. Feel the frequency of this Eclipse shifting the way you view your success, your work, and your time to vibrate to a new level of being, exemplifying the highest vibrations of your North Node.

SOLAR ECLIPSE X CAPRICORN

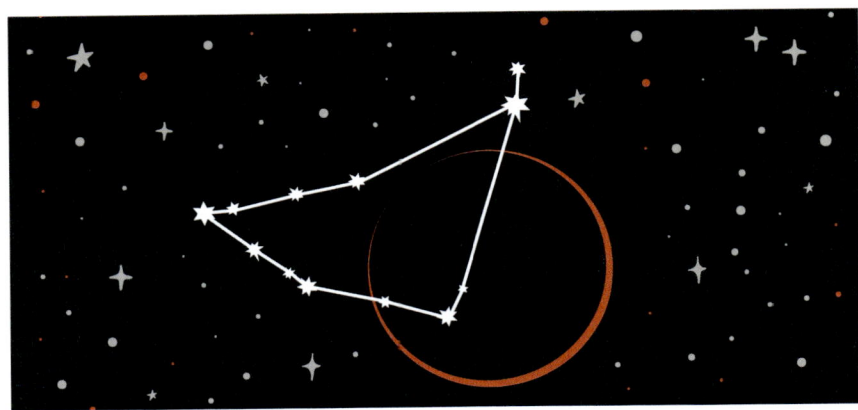

Coming to us just days before the New Year, the Capricorn Solar Eclipse is the perfect time to clarify your focus, intentions and your direction. It is also a time to rest, to prepare for what's ahead, and enjoy what you already worked hard to manifest. This Moon is a time for reflection and a time for envisioning your next future. As you look back on what you've accomplished this year, align with the vibrations of joy and gratitude. See how the dots all connected, even the ones you didn't understand at the time. Feel into what people, situations, and struggles helped you evolve and acknowledge the lessons which supported your unique journey. Taking this time to feel genuinely grateful for all that you've created in your life will raise your vibration and help you effortlessly attract the energy you need in 2020.

As you reflect upon the last year, see where your energy flowed. How did you spend your resources? How did you spend your time? More importantly, look to where you felt the most abundant in your energy. Part of our collective journey from the South Node to the North Node this Solar Eclipse is moving from scarcity to abundance. One of the lower vibrations of Capricorn encourages us to see our time and energy as finite. It compels us to think we have limited resources, and if we choose one thing, we can not have another. While this may make logical sense, it doesn't make energetic sense. When we are aligned with our purpose and our soul, the more energy we spend on something, the more we gain back in return. It's a wonderful circle of reciprocity where we never feel depleted or diminished. It also makes choosing where to place our focus easy. Feel into what nourishes you and makes you feel abundant, in all ways, and that is what is worth your energy.

The key to understanding what feeds our soul is knowing yourself. This New Moon is a time to redefine what brings you joy. This may be your work, it may be a hobby, or a partner, it may even be a walk in the park. Explore what lights you up from the inside and relaxes you. Feel into what puts you in a state of gratitude for yourself and your path. Feel into what reassures your path and lets you know you're headed in the direction of growth. When we feel aligned with our soul's path, we experience joy. Our passions become our purpose, and our purpose becomes our work. We become nourished by our work instead of depleted and can remain in a higher vibratory state. We then can attract the support and resources we need, without

SOLAR ECLIPSE X CAPRICORN

having to force something or expend a lot of energy. Our energetic resources remain abundant, and we, in turn, can give more to others around us. It starts, though, with understanding what keeps us in a high vibration of joy and gratitude.

As you start to clarify what raises your vibration, it will become clear what to call in more of in the new year. Also, feel into what brings you back to your center when you spiraled somewhere else. What brings you back to a state of gratitude? What realigns you with your purpose after you've taken a detour? Look to last year for some clues and examples of what brought you home to yourself after you veered from your path. It's natural for us to wander away from balance every so often; this is what allows us to define balance and create ways to stay there. From time to time, you may have found yourself out of alignment with your center, your values, and what brings you joy. Learn from those experiences and recognize clues that preceded them. Be kind and compassionate with yourself when reviewing your missteps. All of your experiences are part of your path, even the ones that take you far from home. Learn the clues to when you are falling off course, so next time you can readjust more quickly and realign yourself with more ease.

Knowing what raises and lowers our vibration is an important step in our personal growth. It's not always easy to understand how we are affected in the moment, but once we make ourselves aware of every nuance of energy we go through, it becomes easy to identify what drains us, what limits us, what amplifies us, and what makes us feel abundant. This knowledge helps us focus on where to place our energy. It becomes clear what projects, people, and activities are worth our resources. It also helps us develop our life's work in the form of our message, our career, and our mission. Spend time this New Moon asking yourself what raises and what lowers your vibration. This is the first place to start your New Year's intentions and your focus for the rest of the decade.

Aspects

There are a few other influences on this New Moon, other than the Solar Eclipse. Jupiter is conjunct the Moon and the Sun in Capricorn. Jupiter expands our vibration and brings us faith. Its energy inspires us to believe the best will happen if we have the courage to take the leap. Jupiter brings a good feeling vibration to this New Moon and helps us further align with our own joy. Feel into the energy of Jupiter when creating your intentions for the New Year. Harness its power to help you trust in your path and take a leap where you may be feeling stagnant. Assume the best case scenario and replace all of your negative what-ifs with positive ones which encourage you to move forward into expansion.

We also have a trine aspect this New Moon with Uranus. Uranus is adding its vibration of change to this Moon and shaking us out of our old habits. Uranus helps break up stagnant energy, and its influence can often throw us off-center as it pulls us out of patterns. Allow Uranus's energy to teach you that sometimes we need to feel some chaos as all the piece of ourselves get shuffled around to realign with our true self. Allow this energy in your vibration, permitting it to shake up anything which doesn't serve you. If you feel disorganized in your energy and visions for a moment, know that this is just Uranus making waves and redirecting you to brighter seas.

SETTING UP for MAGIC

write down things that
no longer serve you and release
them through fire

write your intentions

sage yourself

use rose oil
place a drop on your forehead
and take savasana

The Solar Eclipse begins at 7:34 PM Pacific Time December 25th, with the maximum Eclipse occurring at 9:17 PM Pacific Time, and ending at 11 PM Pacific Time. For much of the world, the Eclipse will occur on December 26th. Please note that the Eclipse happens at the same moment in time no matter where you are located. The actual time and day may differ, though, depending on your timezone, for instance. The Eclipse occurs at 9:17 PM Pacific Time, 12:17 AM Eastern Time (December 26th), and 5:17 AM UTC (December 26th). These are all the same moment, just at different times. You can choose to practice your rituals during the time of the Eclipse, but for some, this won't be feasible. You can still hold your circles and set your intentions anytime Dec 25th, 26th, or 27th, as the energy of the New Moon will still be available.

A Solar Eclipse Circle is much like a New Moon Circle, except there is an element of release included. Most New Moon circles focus on looking forward with intentions and visions. While an Eclipse circle has these elements, it also provides us a place to cut cords with old patterns so we can make even greater shifts in the upcoming Lunar Cycle. Before beginning your process of release and intention setting, first pick a space that can hold your energy and the energy of anyone practicing with you. This space can be inside or out, just make sure it is well ventilated, so as you release the energy, it has somewhere to go. Also, choose a space that feels grounded and has a stillness when you enter. This can be a room in your home, or you can carve out an energetic space if you are traveling in a hotel room, airplane, or a place in nature.

After you've chosen a space, imagine a white light creating the boundary of the circle, protecting you, and sealing it from other vibrations entering. Incorporate as many of the four elements as possible, representing Earth, through crystals and flowers, Fire, through candles, Air through Auric Sprays and smudge sticks, and Water through room diffusers, or a simple bowl full of water. As you place the items in and around your circle, use your intuition to guide you, knowing there is no "right" or "wrong" way to do this. You may even set up a crystal grid in the center of the circle to anchor and ground

SETTING UP for MAGIC

it in space. Crystal grids are also wonderful ways to direct the energy of the space. You can use the crystals for Capricorn to set up a grid to direct energy to stillness and focus. Know that you can practice with only yourself and this workbook. Nothing else is needed to align with the energy of the day. The other items are just a bonus and help enhance your practice but do not create it. Your willingness to open up, to look within, and expand your consciousness is the most important piece to this day.

The other pieces for calling in and aligning with the energy of Capricorn are listed below. You can combine them in any way you like.

Colors: Dark Greens and grays
Shapes: Square
Texture/Fabric: Dark Woods, like walnut and Petrified Woods.
Scents: Sandalwood, Myrrh, Patchouli
Flowers: Holly, African violet, Pansy

Once you set up your circle, cleanse the space with sage or palo santo. After the circle is cleansed, smudge yourself and your friends before they enter the circle. Begin the circle by acknowledging everyone in the room. Continue to the yoga in this workbook if you are practicing this piece tonight. Yoga is a wonderful way to move your energy before setting intentions and helps clarify your energy by removing stagnant vibrations. Even if you forgo the yoga because of space or some other reason, practice a special ritual for the Eclipse with Rose Oil. Place a small drop of rose oil on the middle of your forehead, where your third eye is located while in Savasana. Rose oil calms the nervous system, which tends to get over-activated during an Eclipse. Keep the Rose Oil on yourself throughout the meditation.

Once you feel centered in your body, begin to write down what you are releasing this day. These can be old habits of your South Node or lower vibrations you align with from Capricorn. They can also be emotions from situations that you've learned from and no longer need in your life. After you've written down your releases, safely burn them. Watch the energy transform into something else as it leaves your field, creating space for new vibrations.

After you've made some space in your frequency continue to understanding the astrological significance of this night and what it means for you. You can do this by journaling it for yourself, or if in a group, you can discuss your experiences with the energy of Capricorn and the Eclipse. Continue to the journal prompts, giving the answers space to appear. Try to receive the answers from your intuitive self, instead of creating them from your logical mind. Once you feel you understand the energies and where they come from, continue to the intention setting portion, again receiving the answers. At this point, you may also pull some cards to help tune further into your intuitive guidance. You can use tarot cards, Goddess cards, animal medicine cards, or any other decks that may be in your toolkit.

Once you've finished the circle, close it with gratitude. Either write down or think to yourself about all that you are thankful for in your life. Thank the space for holding you, and thank yourself for showing up to do the work. You can even practice being grateful for things that haven't come your way yet. Gratitude will attract them to your energy and let the universe know you are ready to receive them. Enjoy this time to be with yourself, your heart, and your soul. Feel the Solar Eclipse shifting your vibration from old endings to new beginnings, rooted in joy.

Lessons from Capricorn:

- the best way to release something is to remove your attention from it.

- your energy is waiting for your direction

- success shows up as joy

- time alone brings out the answers you already know

- spirit daughter

SOLAR ECLIPSE QUESTIONS

The next pages are for you to open up to yourself and receive the answers your soul already knows. Take your time with each question and be as honest with yourself as possible. You can always return to the breath as a resting place. Answer these questions on the day or days around the New Moon. Trust the process.

1. What lessons did 2019 bring you about your life's path?

_____

_____

_____

_____

_____

_____

_____

_____

_____

_____

_____

_____

_____

_____

_____

_____

_____

_____

_____

_____

2. What amplifies your energy? What drains it?
    What reciprocates it?

3. How does it feel to be out of alignment with your center? What brings you back to center?

_____

_____

_____

_____

_____

_____

_____

_____

_____

_____

_____

_____

_____

_____

_____

_____

_____

_____

_____

_____

_____

_____

_____

_____

4. What brings you joy and connects you with your soul?
How can you turn it into your life's work?

INTENTION SETTING

Now is the time to plant your intentions for the next lunar cycle, the next year, and possibly the next decade. Intentions differ from the typical New Year's resolutions in many ways. When we set intentions, we are envisioning a way of life. We create a vision that can manifest through different means. A resolution is a fixed goal, with little wiggle room or improvisation for our intuition. We set resolutions, and often, we set ourselves up for failure with to-do lists. We live intentions. They grow and evolve as we shift. Intentions are more about the journey to achieve them and the energy they attract into our world. Resolutions are concerned with the endpoint and nothing in between.

Every Lunar Cycle brings us the chance to set new intentions for ourselves around the astrological theme of the New Moon. The Capricorn New Moon is no different, but also opens up the possibility of weaving our lunar intentions with our New Year's intentions. Remember, setting intentions not about viewing yourself or your life as a problem waiting to be fixed. They are about helping you live your best life, the one that makes you feel aligned with your soul and its energetic journey.

We are also at the end of a decade with a new one on the horizon. Feel into the immensity of this time, but do not feel pressured by it. You can always change, or shift, any of your intentions at any point. They are here to serve you, not the other way around. As you set your intentions, envision the way you want to feel. Create a scene in your mind. See yourself living a life of focus, aligned with your soul and your life's work. What does this look like? What does it feel like?

On this special New Moon, write many scenes. See yourself a month from now, six months from now on the Full Moon in Capricorn, and even 5 or 10 years from now. Play out a day in your life from each of these times. Write in as much detail as you can. Who are you with? What are you doing? Where are you? Most importantly, focus on feeling. Feel into this life you are envisioning. As you invoke the feelings of your best life, you naturally vibrate to a place where you can attract it. One of the most powerful skills you can develop when setting intentions, is to create a feeling that it has already happened. Try being grateful for your intentions already occurring. If you can feel it, you can live it.

After you set your intentions, revise them as much as you'd like. Review them throughout the month and remember they are not hard, fast goals to achieve. They are a way of life to cultivate and nourish.

INTENTION SETTING

INTENTION SETTING

NEW YEAR
NEW DECADE AFFIRMATIONS

JAN 1ST

Affirmations help you define your energy and tell the universe what you are ready to call into your life. These are potent declarations that provide clarity to your intentions. They bring focus to your frequency and help you send out the vibration you want to attract. They are also helpful reminders throughout your day to tune into the vibration you are capable of achieving. If you feel lost, or uncentered at any time, come back to your affirmations. They will help lead you home.

You can create as many affirmations as you like and have different affirmations for different areas of our life. They can be used to shift your vibration and call in matching frequencies to support you. In the boxes below, write three to five affirmations that help support you in cultivating the energy listed in each box. Affirmations are personal and are born from your intuition. There are no "right" or "wrong" affirmations. Do, though, make them powerful "I am" statements that invoke the feelings listed. As you chose the ones to write, say them to yourself out loud or in your head. Let them reflect different energies and pick the ones which resonate deeply with your soul. Write down the affirmations that feel like home to you. Repeat them daily or when you need to vibrate at a particular frequency.

Separate affirmations for different areas of their life:

FOR SELF-CARE

TO FEEL CONFIDENT
(FOR CONFIDENCE)

TO INSPIRE
(FOR INSPIRATION)

TO ENCOURAGE
(FOR ENCOURAGEMENT)

TO FEEL LOVED
(FOR LOVE)

WAXING MOON

DEC 27TH - JAN 9TH

As the Moon builds light, begin to build your dreams. Challenges and hurdles may pop up during this time of the Lunar Cycle around the intentions you set on the Solar Eclipse. Keep yourself motivated by remembering the energies you already embody, which will help you create your visions. In the bricks below write the vibrations you always carry with you. Examples are: courage, positive thinking, love, compassion, etc. Refer back this page when you need a reminder of your strength and resilience.

WAXING MOON

DEC 27TH - JAN 9TH

TRANSITS

DECEMBER 28TH: MERCURY ENTERS CAPRICORN

Mercury is the planet of communication. It activates our willingness to share and exchange information with others. Mercury's energy is influenced by the astrological sign it sits within, and this influence affects our communication, both with others and ourselves. Mercury in Capricorn helps clarify our speech, our writing, and all other forms of communication. Feel into this vibration as you write your New Year intentions. Become clear with yourself and clear in your commitments to your energy. Mercury in Capricorn, asks:

"How does the verbiage you use affect your vibration?"

JANUARY 2ND: FIRST QUARTER MOON IN ARIES

First Quarter Moons are a time for creating the first steps towards a life based on our intentions. It is often during this time we become discouraged or simply forget the intentions we wrote on the New Moon. Perhaps some initial hurdles have come up, or we have lost the courage we found during the Solar Eclipse. Our old patterns may be holding on, or we have fallen back into behaviors that we've acknowledged no longer serve us. With the First Quarter in Aries, it's time to take action. It's also time to burn through any blocks, knowing that the only real obstacles occur in our mind. Feel into the fiery energy of Aries to motivate you into taking the initial steps needed to manifest your dreams. The First Quarter Moon in Aries asks:

"What is something you can do today that will take you one step closer to living your intention?"

JANUARY 3RD: MARS ENTERS SAGITTARIUS

Mars is the fiery planet of passion. It motivates us and reminds us to align with our self. Mars teaches us what is worth fighting for in this life and what makes us feel alive. In Sagittarius, Mars encourages us to expand our passions. This transit asks us to challenge our truths and decide which ones resonate with our entire being. Mars doesn't allow us to settle for anything beneath our full potential. In Sagittarius, this applies to our willingness to take leaps and bounds into our future. Mars in Sagittarius asks:

"What leap of faith are you capable of making if only you allow yourself to jump?"

JANUARY 10TH: URANUS DIRECT (ALL PLANETS DIRECT)

Uranus stations direct today, meaning all planets are out of retrograde and moving forward. This forward motion brings us motivation and clarity. It may feel like things are moving quickly right now- because they are! Ground your energy through meditation and feel your feet on the ground as you make massive shifts in your life and energy. Lean into this momentum until February 17th when Mercury turns Retrograde. Now is the time to start new projects, pick up ones that may have been forgotten, and make significant progress in manifesting your visions.

JANUARY 10TH: FULL MOON IN CANCER/ PENUMBRAL LUNAR ECLIPSE

Please see the Full Moon in Cancer Workbook

WANING MOON

JAN 11TH - JAN 19TH

RELEASING & FORGIVING

WHAT I MASTERED THIS SEASON:

_____

_____

_____

_____

_____

_____

_____

WHAT I WILL CONTINUE TO WORK ON:

_____

_____

_____

_____

_____

_____

WHAT I FORGAVE THIS SEASON:

_____

_____

_____

_____

_____

_____

_____

My Trip to

_____

Planning The Trip ✈

Things to do before I go

- [ ] _____
- [ ] _____
- [ ] _____
- [ ] _____
- [ ] _____
- [ ] _____
- [ ] _____
- [ ] _____
- [ ] _____
- [ ] _____
- [ ] _____
- [ ] _____
- [ ] _____
- [ ] _____
- [ ] _____

Flights, Hotel and Car Rental Information

_____

_____

_____

_____

_____

Packing List

- [ ] _____
- [ ] _____
- [ ] _____
- [ ] _____
- [ ] _____
- [ ] _____
- [ ] _____
- [ ] _____
- [ ] _____
- [ ] _____
- [ ] _____
- [ ] _____
- [ ] _____
- [ ] _____
- [ ] _____
- [ ] _____
- [ ] _____
- [ ] _____
- [ ] _____
- [ ] _____
- [ ] _____
- [ ] _____
- [ ] _____
- [ ] _____
- [ ] _____
- [ ] _____
- [ ] _____
- [ ] _____
- [ ] _____
- [ ] _____
- [ ] _____
- [ ] _____
- [ ] _____
- [ ] _____
- [ ] _____
- [ ] _____
- [ ] _____
- [ ] _____

What I plan to do on my trip

Miscellaneous Notes

Travel Expenses

Trip To:		
Description	**Estimated**	**Actual**
TOTAL		

My Trip to

_____

Planning The Trip ✈

Things to do before I go

- ☐ _____
- ☐ _____
- ☐ _____
- ☐ _____
- ☐ _____
- ☐ _____
- ☐ _____
- ☐ _____
- ☐ _____
- ☐ _____
- ☐ _____
- ☐ _____
- ☐ _____
- ☐ _____

Flights, Hotel and Car Rental Information

_____

_____

_____

_____

_____

Packing List

- [ ] _____
- [ ] _____
- [ ] _____
- [ ] _____
- [ ] _____
- [ ] _____
- [ ] _____
- [ ] _____
- [ ] _____
- [ ] _____
- [ ] _____
- [ ] _____
- [ ] _____
- [ ] _____
- [ ] _____
- [ ] _____
- [ ] _____
- [ ] _____
- [ ] _____
- [ ] _____

- [ ] _____
- [ ] _____
- [ ] _____
- [ ] _____
- [ ] _____
- [ ] _____
- [ ] _____
- [ ] _____
- [ ] _____
- [ ] _____
- [ ] _____
- [ ] _____
- [ ] _____
- [ ] _____
- [ ] _____
- [ ] _____
- [ ] _____
- [ ] _____
- [ ] _____
- [ ] _____

What I plan to do on my trip

Miscellaneous Notes

Travel Expenses

Trip To:		
Description	**Estimated**	**Actual**
TOTAL		

My Trip to

_____

Planning The Trip ✈

Things to do before I go

- [ ] _____
- [ ] _____
- [ ] _____
- [ ] _____
- [ ] _____
- [ ] _____
- [ ] _____
- [ ] _____
- [ ] _____
- [ ] _____
- [ ] _____
- [ ] _____
- [ ] _____
- [ ] _____

Flights, Hotel and Car Rental Information

_____

_____

_____

_____

_____

Packing List

- [ ] _____
- [ ] _____
- [ ] _____
- [ ] _____
- [ ] _____
- [ ] _____
- [ ] _____
- [ ] _____
- [ ] _____
- [ ] _____
- [ ] _____
- [ ] _____
- [ ] _____
- [ ] _____
- [ ] _____
- [ ] _____
- [ ] _____
- [ ] _____
- [ ] _____
- [ ] _____
- [ ] _____

- [ ] _____
- [ ] _____
- [ ] _____
- [ ] _____
- [ ] _____
- [ ] _____
- [ ] _____
- [ ] _____
- [ ] _____
- [ ] _____
- [ ] _____
- [ ] _____
- [ ] _____
- [ ] _____
- [ ] _____
- [ ] _____
- [ ] _____
- [ ] _____
- [ ] _____
- [ ] _____

What I plan to do on my trip

Miscellaneous Notes

Travel Expenses

Trip To:		
Description	**Estimated**	**Actual**
TOTAL		

My Trip to

_____

Planning The Trip

Things to do before I go

- [ ]
- [ ]
- [ ]
- [ ]
- [ ]
- [ ]
- [ ]
- [ ]
- [ ]
- [ ]
- [ ]
- [ ]
- [ ]
- [ ]

Flights, Hotel and Car Rental Information

Packing List

- [ ] _____
- [ ] _____
- [ ] _____
- [ ] _____
- [ ] _____
- [ ] _____
- [ ] _____
- [ ] _____
- [ ] _____
- [ ] _____
- [ ] _____
- [ ] _____
- [ ] _____
- [ ] _____
- [ ] _____
- [ ] _____
- [ ] _____
- [ ] _____
- [ ] _____
- [ ] _____
- [ ] _____

- [ ] _____
- [ ] _____
- [ ] _____
- [ ] _____
- [ ] _____
- [ ] _____
- [ ] _____
- [ ] _____
- [ ] _____
- [ ] _____
- [ ] _____
- [ ] _____
- [ ] _____
- [ ] _____
- [ ] _____
- [ ] _____
- [ ] _____
- [ ] _____
- [ ] _____
- [ ] _____
- [ ] _____

What I plan to do on my trip

Miscellaneous Notes

Travel Expenses

Trip To:

Description	Estimated	Actual
TOTAL		

My Trip to

_____

Planning The Trip ✈

Things to do before I go

- [ ] _____
- [ ] _____
- [ ] _____
- [ ] _____
- [ ] _____
- [ ] _____
- [ ] _____
- [ ] _____
- [ ] _____
- [ ] _____
- [ ] _____
- [ ] _____
- [ ] _____
- [ ] _____

Flights, Hotel and Car Rental Information

_____

_____

_____

_____

_____

Packing List

- [ ] _____
- [ ] _____
- [ ] _____
- [ ] _____
- [ ] _____
- [ ] _____
- [ ] _____
- [ ] _____
- [ ] _____
- [ ] _____
- [ ] _____
- [ ] _____
- [ ] _____
- [ ] _____
- [ ] _____
- [ ] _____
- [ ] _____
- [ ] _____
- [ ] _____
- [ ] _____

- [ ] _____
- [ ] _____
- [ ] _____
- [ ] _____
- [ ] _____
- [ ] _____
- [ ] _____
- [ ] _____
- [ ] _____
- [ ] _____
- [ ] _____
- [ ] _____
- [ ] _____
- [ ] _____
- [ ] _____
- [ ] _____
- [ ] _____
- [ ] _____
- [ ] _____
- [ ] _____

What I plan to do on my trip

Miscellaneous Notes

Travel Expenses

Trip To:		
Description	**Estimated**	**Actual**
TOTAL		

My Daily Travel Journal

Date/Place/Country

_____

_____

_____

Weather today ☀ 🌤 ⛅ 🌧 🌦 ❄

I woke up today feeling/am grateful for

_____

_____

_____

Important information I need to know

_____

_____

_____

What I want to do today

_____

_____

_____

_____

Favorite place(s) I visited today

_____

_____

Most exciting thing I saw today

_____

_____

_____

Best meals/restaurant of the day

_____

_____

_____

Interesting people I met today and their contact info

_____

_____

What and who I bought gifts for

_____

_____

_____

Thoughts/Memories

_____

_____

_____

_____

_____

_____

_____

_____

_____

My Daily Travel Journal

Date/Place/Country

_____

_____

_____

Weather today

I woke up today feeling/am grateful for

_____

_____

_____

Important information I need to know

_____

_____

_____

What I want to do today

_____

_____

_____

_____

Favorite place(s) I visited today

_____

_____

Most exciting thing I saw today

_____

_____

_____

Best meals/restaurant of the day

_____

_____

_____

Interesting people I met today and their contact info

_____

_____

What and who I bought gifts for

_____

_____

_____

Thoughts/Memories

_____

_____

_____

_____

_____

_____

_____

_____

My Daily Travel Journal

Date/Place/Country

_____

_____

_____

Weather today ☀️ 🌤️ ☁️ 🌧️ ⛈️ ❄️

I woke up today feeling/am grateful for

_____

_____

_____

Important information I need to know

_____

_____

_____

What I want to do today

_____

_____

_____

Favorite place(s) I visited today

_____

Most exciting thing I saw today

_____

_____

_____

Best meals/restaurant of the day

_____

_____

_____

Interesting people I met today and their contact info

_____

_____

What and who I bought gifts for

_____

_____

_____

Thoughts/Memories

_____

_____

_____

_____

_____

_____

_____

_____

_____

My Daily Travel Journal

Date/Place/Country

_____

_____

_____

Weather today ☀️ 🌤️ ⛅ 🌧️ ☁️ ❄️

I woke up today feeling/am grateful for

_____

_____

_____

Important information I need to know

_____

_____

_____

What I want to do today

_____

_____

_____

_____

Favorite place(s) I visited today

_____

_____

Most exciting thing I saw today

_____

_____

_____

Best meals/restaurant of the day

_____

_____

_____

Interesting people I met today and their contact info

_____

_____

What and who I bought gifts for

_____

_____

_____

Thoughts/Memories

_____

_____

_____

_____

_____

_____

_____

_____

_____

My Daily Travel Journal

Date/Place/Country

_____

_____

_____

Weather today ☀️ 🌤️ ☁️ 🌧️ ⛅ ❄️

I woke up today feeling/am grateful for

_____

_____

_____

Important information I need to know

_____

_____

_____

What I want to do today

_____

_____

_____

_____

Favorite place(s) I visited today

_____

_____

Most exciting thing I saw today

_____

_____

_____

Best meals/restaurant of the day

_____

_____

_____

Interesting people I met today and their contact info

_____

_____

What and who I bought gifts for

_____

_____

_____

Thoughts/Memories

_____

_____

_____

_____

_____

_____

_____

_____

_____

My Daily Travel Journal

Date/Place/Country

_____

_____

_____

Weather today ☀️ 🌤️ ⛅ 🌧️ 🌦️ ❄️

I woke up today feeling/am grateful for

_____

_____

_____

Important information I need to know

_____

_____

_____

What I want to do today

_____

_____

_____

Favorite place(s) I visited today

_____

_____

Most exciting thing I saw today

_____

_____

_____

Best meals/restaurant of the day

_____

_____

_____

Interesting people I met today and their contact info

_____

_____

What and who I bought gifts for

_____

_____

_____

Thoughts/Memories

_____

_____

_____

_____

_____

_____

_____

_____

_____

My Daily Travel Journal

Date/Place/Country

_____

_____

_____

Weather today ☀️ ⛅ ☁️ 🌧️ ⛈️ ❄️

I woke up today feeling/am grateful for

_____

_____

_____

Important information I need to know

_____

_____

_____

What I want to do today

_____

_____

_____

_____

Favorite place(s) I visited today

_____

_____

Most exciting thing I saw today

_____

_____

_____

Best meals/restaurant of the day

_____

_____

_____

Interesting people I met today and their contact info

_____

_____

What and who I bought gifts for

_____

_____

_____

Thoughts/Memories

_____

_____

_____

_____

_____

_____

_____

_____

My Daily Travel Journal

Date/Place/Country

_____

_____

_____

Weather today ☀️ 🌤️ ⛅ 🌧️ 🌦️ ❄️

I woke up today feeling/am grateful for

_____

_____

_____

Important information I need to know

_____

_____

_____

What I want to do today

_____

_____

_____

_____

Favorite place(s) I visited today

_____

_____

Most exciting thing I saw today

_____

_____

_____

Best meals/restaurant of the day

_____

_____

_____

Interesting people I met today and their contact info

_____

_____

What and who I bought gifts for

_____

_____

_____

Thoughts/Memories

_____

_____

_____

_____

_____

_____

_____

_____

_____

My Daily Travel Journal

Date/Place/Country

_____

_____

_____

Weather today ☀️ 🌤️ ⛅ 🌧️ ⛈️ ❄️ 🌙

I woke up today feeling/am grateful for

_____

_____

_____

Important information I need to know

_____

_____

_____

What I want to do today

_____

_____

_____

_____

Favorite place(s) I visited today

_____

_____

Most exciting thing I saw today

_____

_____

_____

Best meals/restaurant of the day

_____

_____

_____

Interesting people I met today and their contact info

_____

_____

What and who I bought gifts for

_____

_____

_____

Thoughts/Memories

_____

_____

_____

_____

_____

_____

_____

_____

_____

My Daily Travel Journal

Date/Place/Country

_____

_____

_____

Weather today ☀️ 🌤️ ⛅ 🌧️ ⛈️ ❄️

I woke up today feeling/am grateful for

_____

_____

_____

Important information I need to know

_____

_____

_____

What I want to do today

_____

_____

_____

_____

Favorite place(s) I visited today

_____

_____

Most exciting thing I saw today

_____

_____

_____

Best meals/restaurant of the day

_____

_____

_____

Interesting people I met today and their contact info

_____

_____

What and who I bought gifts for

_____

_____

_____

Thoughts/Memories

_____

_____

_____

_____

_____

_____

_____

_____

My Daily Travel Journal

Date/Place/Country

_____

_____

_____

Weather today ☀️ 🌤️ ⛅ 🌧️ ⛈️ ❄️

I woke up today feeling/am grateful for

_____

_____

_____

Important information I need to know

_____

_____

_____

What I want to do today

_____

_____

_____

_____

Favorite place(s) I visited today

_____

_____

Most exciting thing I saw today

_____

_____

_____

Best meals/restaurant of the day

_____

_____

_____

Interesting people I met today and their contact info

_____

_____

What and who I bought gifts for

_____

_____

_____

Thoughts/Memories

_____

_____

_____

_____

_____

_____

_____

_____

_____

My Daily Travel Journal

Date/Place/Country

_____

_____

_____

Weather today ☀️ 🌤️ ☁️ 🌧️ ⛈️ ❄️

I woke up today feeling/am grateful for

_____

_____

_____

Important information I need to know

_____

_____

_____

What I want to do today

_____

_____

_____

_____

_____

Favorite place(s) I visited today

_____

_____

Most exciting thing I saw today

_____

_____

_____

Best meals/restaurant of the day

_____

_____

_____

Interesting people I met today and their contact info

_____

_____

What and who I bought gifts for

_____

_____

_____

Thoughts/Memories

_____

_____

_____

_____

_____

_____

_____

_____

_____

My Daily Travel Journal

Date/Place/Country

_____

_____

_____

Weather today ☀️ 🌤️ ⛅ 🌧️ 🌧️ ❄️

I woke up today feeling/am grateful for

_____

_____

_____

Important information I need to know

_____

_____

_____

What I want to do today

_____

_____

_____

_____

Favorite place(s) I visited today

_____

_____

Most exciting thing I saw today

_____

_____

_____

Best meals/restaurant of the day

_____

_____

_____

Interesting people I met today and their contact info

_____

_____

What and who I bought gifts for

_____

_____

_____

Thoughts/Memories

_____

_____

_____

_____

_____

_____

_____

_____

_____

My Daily Travel Journal

Date/Place/Country

_____

_____

_____

Weather today

I woke up today feeling/am grateful for

_____

_____

_____

Important information I need to know

_____

_____

_____

What I want to do today

_____

_____

_____

_____

Favorite place(s) I visited today

_____

_____

Most exciting thing I saw today

_____

_____

_____

Best meals/restaurant of the day

_____

_____

_____

Interesting people I met today and their contact info

_____

_____

What and who I bought gifts for

_____

_____

_____

Thoughts/Memories

_____

_____

_____

_____

_____

_____

_____

_____

My Daily Travel Journal

Date/Place/Country

_____

_____

_____

Weather today

I woke up today feeling/am grateful for

_____

_____

_____

Important information I need to know

_____

_____

_____

What I want to do today

_____

_____

_____

_____

Favorite place(s) I visited today

_____

_____

Most exciting thing I saw today

_____

_____

_____

Best meals/restaurant of the day

_____

_____

_____

Interesting people I met today and their contact info

_____

_____

What and who I bought gifts for

_____

_____

_____

Thoughts/Memories

_____

_____

_____

_____

_____

_____

_____

_____

My Daily Travel Journal

Date/Place/Country

_____

_____

_____

Weather today ☀️ 🌤️ ⛅ 🌧️ 🌥️ ❄️

I woke up today feeling/am grateful for

_____

_____

_____

Important information I need to know

_____

_____

_____

What I want to do today

_____

_____

_____

_____

Favorite place(s) I visited today

_____

_____

Most exciting thing I saw today

_____

_____

_____

Best meals/restaurant of the day

_____

_____

_____

Interesting people I met today and their contact info

_____

_____

What and who I bought gifts for

_____

_____

_____

Thoughts/Memories

_____

_____

_____

_____

_____

_____

_____

_____

My Daily Travel Journal

Date/Place/Country

_____

_____

_____

Weather today

I woke up today feeling/am grateful for

_____

_____

_____

Important information I need to know

_____

_____

_____

What I want to do today

_____

_____

_____

Favorite place(s) I visited today

_____

_____

Most exciting thing I saw today

_____

_____

_____

Best meals/restaurant of the day

_____

_____

_____

Interesting people I met today and their contact info

_____

_____

What and who I bought gifts for

_____

_____

_____

Thoughts/Memories

_____

_____

_____

_____

_____

_____

_____

_____

My Daily Travel Journal

Date/Place/Country

_____

_____

_____

Weather today

I woke up today feeling/am grateful for

_____

_____

_____

Important information I need to know

_____

_____

_____

What I want to do today

_____

_____

_____

Favorite place(s) I visited today

_____

_____

Most exciting thing I saw today

_____

_____

_____

Best meals/restaurant of the day

_____

_____

_____

Interesting people I met today and their contact info

_____

_____

What and who I bought gifts for

_____

_____

_____

Thoughts/Memories

_____

_____

_____

_____

_____

_____

_____

_____

My Daily Travel Journal

Date/Place/Country

_____

_____

_____

Weather today ☀️ 🌤️ ⛅ 🌧️ ⛈️ ❄️

I woke up today feeling/am grateful for

_____

_____

_____

Important information I need to know

_____

_____

_____

What I want to do today

_____

_____

_____

_____

Favorite place(s) I visited today

_____

Most exciting thing I saw today

_____

_____

_____

Best meals/restaurant of the day

_____

_____

_____

Interesting people I met today and their contact info

_____

_____

What and who I bought gifts for

_____

_____

_____

Thoughts/Memories

_____

_____

_____

_____

_____

_____

_____

_____

_____

My Daily Travel Journal

Date/Place/Country

_____

_____

_____

Weather today ☀ 🌤 ⛅ 🌧 ⛈ ❄

I woke up today feeling/am grateful for

_____

_____

_____

Important information I need to know

_____

_____

_____

What I want to do today

_____

_____

_____

_____

Favorite place(s) I visited today

_____

_____

Most exciting thing I saw today

_____

_____

_____

Best meals/restaurant of the day

_____

_____

_____

Interesting people I met today and their contact info

_____

_____

What and who I bought gifts for

_____

_____

_____

Thoughts/Memories

_____

_____

_____

_____

_____

_____

_____

_____

My Daily Travel Journal

Date/Place/Country

_____

_____

_____

Weather today

I woke up today feeling/am grateful for

_____

_____

_____

Important information I need to know

_____

_____

_____

What I want to do today

_____

_____

_____

Favorite place(s) I visited today

_____

_____

Most exciting thing I saw today

_____

_____

_____

Best meals/restaurant of the day

_____

_____

_____

Interesting people I met today and their contact info

_____

_____

_____

What and who I bought gifts for

_____

_____

_____

Thoughts/Memories

_____

_____

_____

_____

_____

_____

_____

_____

_____

_____

My Daily Travel Journal

Date/Place/Country

_____

_____

_____

Weather today ☀️ 🌤️ ☁️ 🌧️ ⛅ 🌨️

I woke up today feeling/am grateful for

_____

_____

_____

Important information I need to know

_____

_____

_____

What I want to do today

_____

_____

_____

_____

Favorite place(s) I visited today

_____

_____

Most exciting thing I saw today

_____

_____

_____

Best meals/restaurant of the day

_____

_____

_____

Interesting people I met today and their contact info

_____

_____

What and who I bought gifts for

_____

_____

_____

Thoughts/Memories

_____

_____

_____

_____

_____

_____

_____

_____

My Daily Travel Journal

Date/Place/Country

_____

_____

_____

Weather today

I woke up today feeling/am grateful for

_____

_____

_____

Important information I need to know

_____

_____

_____

What I want to do today

_____

_____

_____

Favorite place(s) I visited today

_____

_____

Most exciting thing I saw today

_____

_____

_____

Best meals/restaurant of the day

_____

_____

_____

Interesting people I met today and their contact info

_____

_____

What and who I bought gifts for

_____

_____

_____

Thoughts/Memories

_____

_____

_____

_____

_____

_____

_____

_____

_____

My Daily Travel Journal

Date/Place/Country

_____

_____

_____

Weather today ☀️ 🌤️ ☁️ 🌧️ ⛈️ ❄️

I woke up today feeling/am grateful for

_____

_____

_____

Important information I need to know

_____

_____

_____

What I want to do today

_____

_____

_____

Favorite place(s) I visited today

_____

_____

Most exciting thing I saw today

_____

_____

_____

Best meals/restaurant of the day

_____

_____

_____

Interesting people I met today and their contact info

_____

_____

What and who I bought gifts for

_____

_____

_____

Thoughts/Memories

_____

_____

_____

_____

_____

_____

_____

_____

_____

My Daily Travel Journal

Date/Place/Country

_____

_____

_____

Weather today

I woke up today feeling/am grateful for

_____

_____

_____

Important information I need to know

_____

_____

_____

What I want to do today

_____

_____

_____

Favorite place(s) I visited today

_____

_____

Most exciting thing I saw today

_____

_____

_____

Best meals/restaurant of the day

_____

_____

_____

Interesting people I met today and their contact info

_____

_____

What and who I bought gifts for

_____

_____

_____

Thoughts/Memories

_____

_____

_____

_____

_____

_____

_____

_____

My Daily Travel Journal

Date/Place/Country

_____

_____

_____

Weather today ☀️ 🌤️ ☁️ 🌧️ ☁️ ❄️

I woke up today feeling/am grateful for

_____

_____

_____

Important information I need to know

_____

_____

_____

What I want to do today

_____

_____

_____

Favorite place(s) I visited today

_____

_____

Most exciting thing I saw today

_____

_____

_____

Best meals/restaurant of the day

_____

_____

_____

Interesting people I met today and their contact info

_____

_____

What and who I bought gifts for

_____

_____

_____

Thoughts/Memories

_____

_____

_____

_____

_____

_____

_____

_____

My Daily Travel Journal

Date/Place/Country

_____

_____

_____

Weather today

I woke up today feeling/am grateful for

_____

_____

_____

Important information I need to know

_____

_____

_____

What I want to do today

_____

_____

_____

_____

Favorite place(s) I visited today

_____

_____

Most exciting thing I saw today

_____

_____

_____

Best meals/restaurant of the day

_____

_____

_____

Interesting people I met today and their contact info

_____

_____

What and who I bought gifts for

_____

_____

_____

Thoughts/Memories

_____

_____

_____

_____

_____

_____

_____

_____

_____

My Daily Travel Journal

Date/Place/Country

_____

_____

_____

Weather today

I woke up today feeling/am grateful for

_____

_____

_____

Important information I need to know

_____

_____

_____

What I want to do today

_____

_____

_____

Favorite place(s) I visited today

_____

_____

Most exciting thing I saw today

_____

_____

_____

Best meals/restaurant of the day

_____

_____

_____

Interesting people I met today and their contact info

_____

_____

What and who I bought gifts for

_____

_____

_____

Thoughts/Memories

_____

_____

_____

_____

_____

_____

_____

_____

My Daily Travel Journal

Date/Place/Country

_____

_____

_____

Weather today ☀ ⛅ ☁ 🌧 🌥 ❄

I woke up today feeling/am grateful for

_____

_____

_____

Important information I need to know

_____

_____

_____

What I want to do today

_____

_____

_____

_____

Favorite place(s) I visited today

_____

_____

Most exciting thing I saw today

_____

_____

_____

Best meals/restaurant of the day

_____

_____

_____

Interesting people I met today and their contact info

_____

_____

What and who I bought gifts for

_____

_____

_____

Thoughts/Memories

_____

_____

_____

_____

_____

_____

_____

_____

_____

My Daily Travel Journal

Date/Place/Country

_____

_____

_____

Weather today ☀ 🌤 ⛅ 🌧 ☁ ❄

I woke up today feeling/am grateful for

_____

_____

_____

Important information I need to know

_____

_____

_____

What I want to do today

_____

_____

_____

Favorite place(s) I visited today

_____

_____

Most exciting thing I saw today

_____

_____

_____

Best meals/restaurant of the day

_____

_____

_____

Interesting people I met today and their contact info

_____

_____

What and who I bought gifts for

_____

_____

_____

Thoughts/Memories

_____

_____

_____

_____

_____

_____

_____

_____

My Daily Travel Journal

Date/Place/Country

_____

_____

_____

Weather today

I woke up today feeling/am grateful for

_____

_____

_____

Important information I need to know

_____

_____

_____

What I want to do today

_____

_____

_____

Favorite place(s) I visited today

_____

_____

Most exciting thing I saw today

_____

_____

_____

Best meals/restaurant of the day

_____

_____

_____

Interesting people I met today and their contact info

_____

_____

What and who I bought gifts for

_____

_____

_____

Thoughts/Memories

_____

_____

_____

_____

_____

_____

_____

_____

My Daily Travel Journal

Date/Place/Country

_____

_____

_____

Weather today ☀️ ⛅ ☁️ 🌧️ 🌦️ ❄️

I woke up today feeling/am grateful for

_____

_____

_____

Important information I need to know

_____

_____

_____

What I want to do today

_____

_____

_____

_____

Favorite place(s) I visited today

_____

_____

Most exciting thing I saw today

_____

_____

_____

Best meals/restaurant of the day

_____

_____

_____

Interesting people I met today and their contact info

_____

_____

What and who I bought gifts for

_____

_____

_____

Thoughts/Memories

_____

_____

_____

_____

_____

_____

_____

_____

_____

My Daily Travel Journal

Date/Place/Country

_____

_____

_____

Weather today

I woke up today feeling/am grateful for

_____

_____

_____

Important information I need to know

_____

_____

_____

What I want to do today

_____

_____

_____

Favorite place(s) I visited today

_____

_____

Most exciting thing I saw today

_____

_____

_____

Best meals/restaurant of the day

_____

_____

_____

Interesting people I met today and their contact info

_____

_____

What and who I bought gifts for

_____

_____

_____

Thoughts/Memories

_____

_____

_____

_____

_____

_____

_____

_____

_____

My Daily Travel Journal

Date/Place/Country

_____

_____

_____

Weather today ☀️ 🌤️ ⛅ 🌧️ 🌧️ ❄️

I woke up today feeling/am grateful for

_____

_____

_____

Important information I need to know

_____

_____

_____

What I want to do today

_____

_____

_____

Favorite place(s) I visited today

_____

_____

Most exciting thing I saw today

_____

_____

_____

Best meals/restaurant of the day

_____

_____

Interesting people I met today and their contact info

_____

_____

What and who I bought gifts for

_____

_____

_____

Thoughts/Memories

_____

_____

_____

_____

_____

_____

_____

_____

My Daily Travel Journal

Date/Place/Country

_____

_____

_____

Weather today ☀ 🌤 ☁ 🌧 ⛈ ❄

I woke up today feeling/am grateful for

_____

_____

_____

Important information I need to know

_____

_____

_____

What I want to do today

_____

_____

_____

_____

Favorite place(s) I visited today

_____

_____

Most exciting thing I saw today

_____

_____

_____

Best meals/restaurant of the day

_____

_____

_____

Interesting people I met today and their contact info

_____

_____

What and who I bought gifts for

_____

_____

_____

Thoughts/Memories

_____

_____

_____

_____

_____

_____

_____

_____

My Daily Travel Journal

Date/Place/Country

Weather today ☀️ ⛅ ☁️ 🌧️ ⛈️ ❄️

I woke up today feeling/am grateful for

Important information I need to know

What I want to do today

Favorite place(s) I visited today

Most exciting thing I saw today

_____

_____

_____

Best meals/restaurant of the day

_____

_____

_____

Interesting people I met today and their contact info

_____

_____

What and who I bought gifts for

_____

_____

_____

Thoughts/Memories

_____

_____

_____

_____

_____

_____

_____

_____

_____

My Daily Travel Journal

Date/Place/Country

_____

_____

_____

Weather today

I woke up today feeling/am grateful for

_____

_____

_____

Important information I need to know

_____

_____

_____

What I want to do today

_____

_____

_____

Favorite place(s) I visited today

_____

_____

Most exciting thing I saw today

_____

_____

_____

Best meals/restaurant of the day

_____

_____

_____

Interesting people I met today and their contact info

_____

_____

What and who I bought gifts for

_____

_____

_____

Thoughts/Memories

_____

_____

_____

_____

_____

_____

_____

_____

My Daily Travel Journal

Date/Place/Country

_____

_____

_____

Weather today

I woke up today feeling/am grateful for

_____

_____

_____

Important information I need to know

_____

_____

_____

What I want to do today

_____

_____

_____

Favorite place(s) I visited today

_____

_____

Most exciting thing I saw today

_____

_____

_____

Best meals/restaurant of the day

_____

_____

_____

Interesting people I met today and their contact info

_____

_____

What and who I bought gifts for

_____

_____

_____

Thoughts/Memories

_____

_____

_____

_____

_____

_____

_____

_____

_____

My Daily Travel Journal

Date/Place/Country

_____

_____

_____

Weather today ☀ ⛅ ☁ 🌧 ⛈ ❄

I woke up today feeling/am grateful for

_____

_____

_____

Important information I need to know

_____

_____

_____

What I want to do today

_____

_____

_____

_____

Favorite place(s) I visited today

_____

_____

Most exciting thing I saw today

_____

_____

_____

Best meals/restaurant of the day

_____

_____

_____

Interesting people I met today and their contact info

_____

_____

What and who I bought gifts for

_____

_____

_____

Thoughts/Memories

_____

_____

_____

_____

_____

_____

_____

_____

My Daily Travel Journal

Date/Place/Country

_____

_____

_____

Weather today

I woke up today feeling/am grateful for

_____

_____

_____

Important information I need to know

_____

_____

_____

What I want to do today

_____

_____

_____

Favorite place(s) I visited today

_____

_____

Most exciting thing I saw today

_____

_____

_____

Best meals/restaurant of the day

_____

_____

_____

Interesting people I met today and their contact info

_____

_____

What and who I bought gifts for

_____

_____

_____

Thoughts/Memories

_____

_____

_____

_____

_____

_____

_____

_____

My Daily Travel Journal

Date/Place/Country

_____

_____

_____

Weather today ☀ ⛅ ☁ 🌧 🌥 ❄

I woke up today feeling/am grateful for

_____

_____

_____

Important information I need to know

_____

_____

_____

What I want to do today

_____

_____

_____

_____

Favorite place(s) I visited today

_____

_____

Most exciting thing I saw today

_____

_____

_____

Best meals/restaurant of the day

_____

_____

_____

Interesting people I met today and their contact info

_____

_____

What and who I bought gifts for

_____

_____

_____

Thoughts/Memories

_____

_____

_____

_____

_____

_____

_____

_____

_____

My Daily Travel Journal

Date/Place/Country

_____

_____

_____

Weather today

I woke up today feeling/am grateful for

_____

_____

_____

Important information I need to know

_____

_____

_____

What I want to do today

_____

_____

_____

Favorite place(s) I visited today

_____

_____

Most exciting thing I saw today

_____

_____

_____

Best meals/restaurant of the day

_____

_____

_____

Interesting people I met today and their contact info

_____

_____

What and who I bought gifts for

_____

_____

_____

Thoughts/Memories

_____

_____

_____

_____

_____

_____

_____

_____

_____

My Daily Travel Journal

Date/Place/Country

_____

_____

_____

Weather today

I woke up today feeling/am grateful for

_____

_____

_____

Important information I need to know

_____

_____

_____

What I want to do today

_____

_____

_____

Favorite place(s) I visited today

_____

_____

Most exciting thing I saw today

_____

_____

_____

Best meals/restaurant of the day

_____

_____

_____

Interesting people I met today and their contact info

_____

_____

What and who I bought gifts for

_____

_____

_____

Thoughts/Memories

_____

_____

_____

_____

_____

_____

_____

_____

My Daily Travel Journal

Date/Place/Country

_____

_____

_____

Weather today ☀️ 🌤️ ☁️ 🌧️ ⛅ ❄️

I woke up today feeling/am grateful for

_____

_____

_____

Important information I need to know

_____

_____

_____

What I want to do today

_____

_____

_____

Favorite place(s) I visited today

_____

_____

Most exciting thing I saw today

_____

_____

_____

Best meals/restaurant of the day

_____

_____

_____

Interesting people I met today and their contact info

_____

_____

What and who I bought gifts for

_____

_____

_____

Thoughts/Memories

_____

_____

_____

_____

_____

_____

_____

_____

My Daily Travel Journal

Date/Place/Country

_____

_____

_____

Weather today ☀️ ⛅ ☁️ 🌧️ 🌥️ ❄️

I woke up today feeling/am grateful for

_____

_____

_____

Important information I need to know

_____

_____

_____

What I want to do today

_____

_____

_____

Favorite place(s) I visited today

_____

_____

Most exciting thing I saw today

_____

_____

_____

Best meals/restaurant of the day

_____

_____

_____

Interesting people I met today and their contact info

_____

_____

What and who I bought gifts for

_____

_____

_____

Thoughts/Memories

_____

_____

_____

_____

_____

_____

_____

_____

My Daily Travel Journal

Date/Place/Country

_____

_____

_____

Weather today ☀️ ⛅ ☁️ 🌧️ 🌧️ ❄️

I woke up today feeling/am grateful for

_____

_____

_____

Important information I need to know

_____

_____

_____

What I want to do today

_____

_____

_____

Favorite place(s) I visited today

_____

_____

Most exciting thing I saw today

_____

_____

_____

Best meals/restaurant of the day

_____

_____

_____

Interesting people I met today and their contact info

_____

_____

What and who I bought gifts for

_____

_____

_____

Thoughts/Memories

_____

_____

_____

_____

_____

_____

_____

_____

My Daily Travel Journal

Date/Place/Country

_____

_____

_____

Weather today ☀️ 🌤️ ⛅ 🌧️ 🌥️ ❄️

I woke up today feeling/am grateful for

_____

_____

_____

Important information I need to know

_____

_____

_____

What I want to do today

_____

_____

_____

Favorite place(s) I visited today

_____

_____

Most exciting thing I saw today

_____

_____

_____

Best meals/restaurant of the day

_____

_____

_____

Interesting people I met today and their contact info

_____

_____

What and who I bought gifts for

_____

_____

_____

Thoughts/Memories

_____

_____

_____

_____

_____

_____

_____

_____

_____

My Daily Travel Journal

Date/Place/Country

_____

_____

_____

Weather today ☀ 🌤 ☁ 🌧 ⛈ ❄

I woke up today feeling/am grateful for

_____

_____

_____

Important information I need to know

_____

_____

_____

What I want to do today

_____

_____

_____

Favorite place(s) I visited today

_____

_____

Most exciting thing I saw today

_____

_____

_____

Best meals/restaurant of the day

_____

_____

_____

Interesting people I met today and their contact info

_____

_____

What and who I bought gifts for

_____

_____

_____

Thoughts/Memories

_____

_____

_____

_____

_____

_____

_____

_____

My Daily Travel Journal

Date/Place/Country

_____

_____

_____

Weather today

I woke up today feeling/am grateful for

_____

_____

_____

Important information I need to know

_____

_____

_____

What I want to do today

_____

_____

_____

Favorite place(s) I visited today

_____

Most exciting thing I saw today

_____

_____

_____

Best meals/restaurant of the day

_____

_____

_____

Interesting people I met today and their contact info

_____

_____

What and who I bought gifts for

_____

_____

_____

Thoughts/Memories

_____

_____

_____

_____

_____

_____

_____

_____

My Daily Travel Journal

Date/Place/Country

_____

_____

_____

Weather today   ☀ ⛅ ☁ 🌧 🌧 ❄

I woke up today feeling/am grateful for

_____

_____

_____

Important information I need to know

_____

_____

_____

What I want to do today

_____

_____

_____

Favorite place(s) I visited today

_____

_____

Most exciting thing I saw today

_____

_____

_____

Best meals/restaurant of the day

_____

_____

_____

Interesting people I met today and their contact info

_____

_____

What and who I bought gifts for

_____

_____

_____

Thoughts/Memories

_____

_____

_____

_____

_____

_____

_____

_____

_____

Attach photos/tickets/receipts/
souvenirs/sketches

Attach photos/tickets/receipts/
souvenirs/sketches

Attach photos/tickets/receipts/
souvenirs/sketches

Attach photos/tickets/receipts/
souvenirs/sketches

Attach photos/tickets/receipts/ souvenirs/sketches

Attach photos/tickets/receipts/
souvenirs/sketches

Attach photos/tickets/receipts/
souvenirs/sketches

©Dartan Creations Ltd.
www.blankbookbillionaire.com

Made in the USA
Lexington, KY
10 December 2019

58383208R00079